Ladybird Readers

The Magic Finger

Series Editor: Sorrel Pitts
Text adapted by R.J. Corrall
Activities written by Catrin Morris
With thanks to Michelle Porte-Davies

LADYBIRD BOOKS

UK | USA | Canada | Ireland | Australia
India | New Zealand | South Africa

Ladybird Books is part of the Penguin Random House group of companies
whose addresses can be found at global.penguinrandomhouse.com.
www.penguin.co.uk   www.puffin.co.uk   www.ladybird.co.uk

Adapted from *The Magic Finger*, first published by Puffin Books, 1966
This version published by Ladybird Books Ltd, 2020
001

Printed in China

The authorized representative in the EEA is Penguin Random House Ireland,
Morrison Chambers, 32 Nassau Street, Dublin D02 YH68

A CIP catalogue record for this book is available from the British Library

ISBN: 978-0-241-54361-0

All correspondence to:
Ladybird Books
Penguin Random House Children's
One Embassy Gardens, 8 Viaduct Gardens, London SW11 7BW

Ladybird Readers

Roald Dahl

The Magic Finger

Based on the original title
by Roald Dahl
Illustrated by Quentin Blake

Picture words

The Magic Finger

Mr. Gregg

Mrs. Gregg

Philip

William

nest

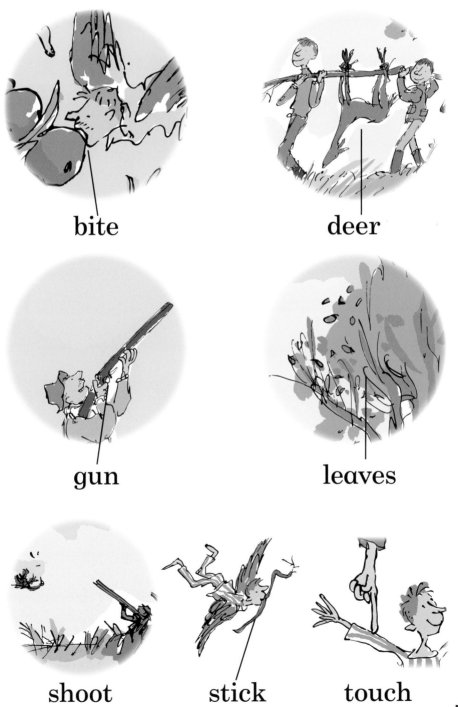

bite

deer

gun

leaves

shoot

stick

touch

I have a Magic Finger.

When I get angry, I get very hot . . .

The first finger of my right hand begins to feel very strange.

A bright light comes out of it and touches the person who made me angry . . .

and then things begin to happen!

I was in a spelling class once when my teacher Mrs. Winter said, "Stand up and spell cat."

"K-a-t," I said.

"You are a naughty little girl!" Mrs. Winter said.

"No, I am not!" I said, angrily.
Then, I pointed the Magic Finger
at Mrs. Winter . . .

and suddenly she had long hairs on
her nose, like a cat!

All the children in the class laughed.

Then, Mrs. Winter turned
around . . . and she had a tail!

She was never the same again
after that.

Last week, I pointed the
Magic Finger at the Gregg family.
Mr. and Mrs. Gregg, and their sons
Philip and William, live next to
our farm.

Philip and William are my friends,
but they like shooting birds and
animals with their father. I HATE it
when they do that.

On Saturday, they shot a beautiful deer. When I saw it, I was very angry. I shouted at Philip and William, but they only laughed . . .

Then, I pointed the Magic Finger at them all.

That afternoon, Mr. Gregg and Philip and William went out again to shoot some ducks.

In the first hour, they shot ten birds. In the next hour, they shot another six.

Then, they saw four more ducks.

They tried to shoot those ducks, too,
but they COULD NOT kill them.
It was very strange—but they could
not hit them.

The Greggs tried again and again,
but the ducks did not stop flying
around their heads.

The next morning, things got stranger. When Mr. Gregg woke up, he could not feel his hands.

He jumped out of bed and saw that he was a very small man now. He did not have arms—he had wings!

Then, Mrs. Gregg jumped out of bed. She was also very small now, and she had wings, too.

"What's happened to us?" she cried.

Philip and William flew into
Mr. and Mrs. Gregg's room—and
they were REALLY small.

"Look at us!" the boys said.
"We can fly!"

Then, they flew out of the window.

Mr. and Mrs. Gregg followed them, and soon all the Greggs were flying around together.

"This is lovely!" they said, but then Philip suddenly called, "Look! Someone is in our garden!"

They all looked down, and they saw four very big ducks. The ducks were as big as men, and they had arms, not wings. They went into the Greggs' house and closed the door.

"They've taken our house!"
Mrs. Gregg said, and she began to
cry. "Where are we going to sleep?"

"Don't cry," Mr. Gregg said.
"We can build a nest!"

The Greggs flew to the top of a
tall tree.

"Now, bring lots of sticks and leaves," said Mr. Gregg. They worked very hard, and they built a beautiful nest.

"It's lovely!" said Mrs. Gregg. "Oh, but what can we have for dinner?"

"We'll fly into our house through an open window and get some biscuits," said Mr. Gregg.

They arrived at the house, but all the windows and doors were closed.

"Look at that duck in our kitchen!" cried Mrs. Gregg.

"Look at that duck with my gun!" said Mr. Gregg.

"There's a duck in my bed!"
shouted William.

"A duck is playing with my
toy train!" said Philip.

The Greggs flew back to their nest.

"What are we going to eat NOW?" said the boys, hungrily.

"We have lots of apple trees in our garden!" said Mr. Gregg. "We can eat apples! Come on!"

It is not easy to eat an apple without hands, but they all had a few bites. Then, they flew back to the nest and tried to sleep.

That night, it was very windy
and very wet.

It was a bad, bad night.

At last, the morning came . . . but when Mr. and Mrs. Gregg looked over the side of the nest, they saw the four ducks on the ground below.

Three of them had the Greggs' guns, and the guns were all pointing at the nest.

"Don't shoot!" Mr. and Mrs. Gregg shouted. "Our two little children are here with us."

"You shot MY six children yesterday," said one of the ducks.

"If you put down your guns,"
said Mr. Gregg, "I will never shoot
a duck again."

"REALLY?" said the duck.

"Yes," said Mr. Gregg. "I will break
the guns into small pieces."

"OK," said the duck. "You can come down."

Then, the Greggs flew out of the nest.

They flew down, down . . .
and suddenly they were in
their garden.

"Our wings have gone!"
said Mr. Gregg.

"We are not small!" laughed
Mrs. Gregg.

Half an hour later, I arrived at the Greggs' farm. I was very surprised when I saw them.

Mr. Gregg was breaking his gun and his boys' guns into pieces.

Philip and William were giving food
to all the birds in the garden.

"What happened?" I asked.

Philip and William told me their story. "Look at our nest!" they said. "We slept there last night."

"We built it," said Mr. Gregg, happily. "Every stick—and we have changed our name. We are not the Gregg family. We are the Egg family, because we love birds now!"

Activities

The key below describes the skills practiced in each activity.

Spelling and writing

Reading

Speaking

Critical thinking

Preparation for the Cambridge Young Learners exams

1 Match the words to the pictures.

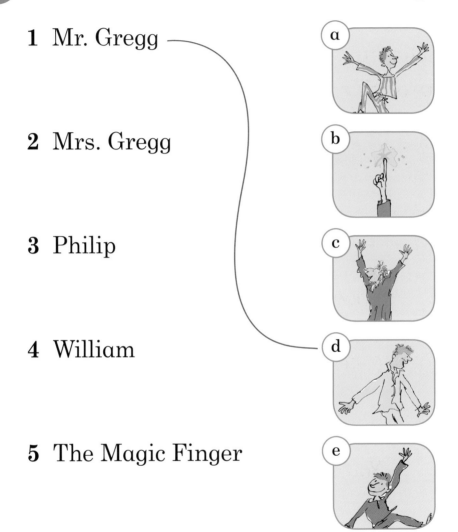

1 Mr. Gregg   a

2 Mrs. Gregg   b

3 Philip   c

4 William   d

5 The Magic Finger   e

2 Look and read. Put a ✓ or a ✗ in the boxes.

1 This is a duck. ✗

2 These are leaves. ☐

3 This is a nest. ☐

4 This is a gun. ☐

5 These are sticks. ☐

3 Ask and answer the questions with a friend. 💬 ❓

I have a Magic Finger.

When I get angry, I get very hot . . .

The first finger of my right hand begins to feel very strange.

A bright light comes out of it and touches the person who made me angry . . .

and then things begin to happen!

6

7

1 What does the girl in the story have?

She has a Magic Finger.

2 Which finger is it?

3 What can it do?

4 When does it happen?

4 Can you remember?
Choose the correct words. 📖

1 My teacher Mrs. Winter said,
  a "Sit down and spell cat."
  b "Stand up and spell cat."

2 Mrs. Winter said,
  a "You are a naughty little girl!"
  b "You are a good girl!"

3 I said, angrily,
  a "No, I am not!"
  b "Yes, I am!"

4 Suddenly she had
  a long hairs on her nose.
  b long hairs on her feet.

5 Find the words.

```
a  w  r  q  s  d  u  c  k  s  h  s
i  k  o  i  n  g  s  g  k  o  s  u
l  s  b  r  q  s  n  e  s  t  p  h
k  e  o  w  o  p  h  s  b  m  o  k
i  x  n  l  e  a  v  e  s  d  h  y
w  i  n  g  s  e  m  g  e  g  u  n
x  s  a  x  o  l  l  e  e  v  e  g
k  h  s  t  i  p  k  d  a  v  p  s
p  d  t  m  k  i  n  g  h  g  k  h
s  e  l  s  g  o  p  h  s  b  m  o
t  e  w  h  s  t  i  c  k  v  u  o
v  r  x  s  a  x  o  l  l  e  h  t
```

deer

ducks

gun

leaves

nest

shoot

stick

wings

6 **Read the text. Write some words to complete the sentences.**

> Last week, I pointed the Magic Finger at the Gregg family.
>
> Philip and William are my friends, but they like shooting animals with their father. On Saturday, they shot a beautiful deer.

1 The girl pointed her

.....Magic Finger..... at her friends.

2 She doesn't like them

.... animals.

3 On Saturday, they shot a

....

7 **Write the questions. Then, write the answers.** 📖 ✏️

1 (did) (family) (Gregg) (shoot) (the)
(What) (?)

Question: What did the Gregg family shoot?

Answer: They shot some ducks.

2 (did) (How) (they) (many) (shoot) (?)

Question: _____

Answer: _____

3 (did) (ducks) (fly) (other) (the)
(Where) (?)

Question: _____

Answer: _____

8 **Complete the sentences.
Write a—d.** 📖

1 The next morning, ...d.......

2 When Mr. Gregg woke up, ...

3 He jumped out of bed and saw ....

4 He did not have arms— ....

---

a he could not feel his hands.

b he had wings!

c that he was a very small man now.

d things got stranger.

9 **Can you remember?**
Choose the correct words.

1 Mrs. Gregg jumped out of
   (**a** bed.)   **b** the nest.

2 She had
   a leaves.   **b** wings.

3 Philip and William were really
   a big.   **b** small.

4 They could
   a fly.   **b** swim.

Look and read. Write *true* or *false*.

Mr. and Mrs. Gregg followed them, and soon all the Greggs were flying around together.

"This is lovely!" they said, but then Philip suddenly called, "Look! Someone is in our garden!"

They all looked down, and they saw four very big ducks. The ducks were as big as men, and they had arms, not wings. They went into the Greggs' house and closed the door.

22

23

1 The Greggs were flying around together.   true

2 They didn't like flying.

3 They saw someone in their garden.

4 There were four ducks in their house.

5 The ducks were smaller than people.

11 Can you remember?
Write the correct form of
the verbs. 📖 ✏️

"They've ___taken___ **(take)** our house!" Mrs. Gregg said, and she _____ **(begin)** to cry. "Where are we going to _____ **(sleep)**?"

" _____ **(not cry)**," Mr. Gregg said. "We can build a nest!"

The Greggs _____ **(fly)** to the top of a tall tree.

12 **Circle the correct pictures.**

1 This can do magic.

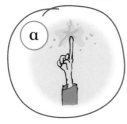 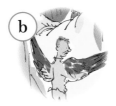 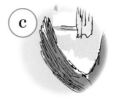

2 This can kill.

3 You can use these to make a nest.

4 This person shoots birds.

13 **Look at the letters. Write the words.** 📖 ✏️ ✿

a e e l s v

1 "Now, bring lots of sticks and leaves," said Mr. Gregg.

s n e t

2 They worked very hard, and they built a beautiful _____.

n i n e d r

3 "It's lovely!" said Mrs. Gregg. "Oh, but what can we have for _____?"

d i w n o w

4 "We'll fly into our house through an open _____ and get some biscuits," said Mr. Gregg.

14 Write *at*, *in*, or *with*.

1 They arrived ..at.. the house, but all the windows and doors were closed.

2 "Look at that duck .... our kitchen!" cried Mrs. Gregg.

3 "Look at that duck .... my gun!" said Mr. Gregg.

4 "There's a duck .... my bed!" shouted William.

5 "A duck is playing .... my toy train!" said Philip.

15 Talk about the two pictures with a friend. How are they different?

a

That afternoon, Mr. Gregg and Philip and William went out again to shoot some ducks.

In the first hour, they shot ten birds. In the next hour, they shot another six.

Then, they saw four more ducks.

14

b

"Don't shoot!" Mr. and Mrs. Gregg shouted. "Our two little children are here with us."

"You shot MY six children yesterday," said one of the ducks.

36

37

In picture a, the Gregg family are shooting at the ducks. In picture b, the ducks are holding the guns.

16 **Look and read. Choose the correct words and write them on the lines.** 📖 ✏️ ⬡

deer	nest	bite

1 A beautiful animal that lives in the country. .... deer ....

2 You can do this to an apple. ....

3 Birds usually live here. ....

17 Order the story. Write *First, Next, After that,* and *Finally.* 📖 ✏️

> The Gregg family shot a lot of ducks.
>
> They agreed never to kill birds again.
>
> They got small, grew wings, and lost their house.
>
> They built a nest.

First, the Gregg family shot a lot of ducks.

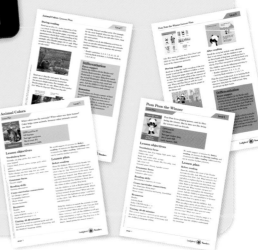